'Nowhere else in England, save at Durham, is there a block of buildings so stately, so beautiful, and so well designed for active church use as the Church, College and Palace, which lie by the bank of the Medway in the old county town.' (so states a guide book of the district ninety years ago). A popular subject with the early postcard photographers, this cluster of buildings, situated on high ground known as the 'Cliff', just off Mill Street, has been the nucleus of Maidstone since the 14th century.

With the authorisation of Richard II, the Archbishop of Canterbury, William Courtenay, pulled down an earlier church of St Mary and commenced building the collegiate church of All Saints in 1395. It is still possible to see some of the stone from St Mary's in the west wall of the present church. All Saints is one of the largest and finest examples of a perpendicular church in England with the nave measuring 93ft in width, and the overall length 227ft. The church formerly had a 100ft wooden spire which was struck by lightning and demolished in 1730.

All Saints was restored in 1886 by J.L. Pearson R.A. at a cost of £12,000 and the internal appearance was greatly changed. This postcard shows the interior of All Saints in 1910. Of interest in the church are:— Archbishop Courtenay's memorial slab (1396) between the choir stalls; the altar tomb (1417) of John Wotton, first master of the College of Priests; the Beale brass (1593); the burial place of Richard Woodville, forbear of Elizabeth, Queen of Edward IV; the Jacobean font, displaying both the Royal Arms and the Arms of Maidstone; and the Lawrence Washington mural tablet that bears the Stars and Stripes of the Washington family, afterwards adopted in the Arms of the U.S.A. According to the 19th century architect, John Whichcord Sen., the County Surveyor and twice Mayor of Maidstone, the original medieval altar stone of Kentish rag lies in the pavement under the east window.

Archbishops Palace, Maidstone.

The Archbishop's Palace dates back to 1348 when the building was commenced by Archbishop Ufford and completed later by Archbishop Islip with the materials from a palace at Wrotham. King Henry VI stayed at the Maidstone Palace on 21st March 1438. The building was improved by Archbishops Morton and Warham at the end of the 15th century and the latter's Coat of Arms can be seen on some of the fireplaces. The Palace passed to Henry VIII in 1537 and ceased to have any connection with the ecclesiastical foundation. At different periods it belonged to the ill-fated Sir Thomas Wyatt, members of the Astley family, who added the Elizabethan front, and Lord Romney. By 1887 the building had fallen into decay and was due for demolition and the erection in its place of warehouses and cottages. Fortunately it was rescued from destruction by public subscription, to be used for civic activities by the people of Maidstone as a permanent memorial of Queen Victoria's Golden Jubilee. The old Palace, a medley of restorations and alterations is currently undergoing extensive renovation.

The Archbishop's Stables or Tithe Barn, dating from the 14th century, probably provided accommodation, on the top floor, for the servants and grooms at the Palace or College. Two noteworthy features of the building are the crown post roof and the early external staircase. This postcard was photographed shortly after the Corporation purchased the Stables in 1913. During World War I the building was converted into a small munitions factory where several girls were employed. The premises are now devoted to an exhibition of carriages and accessories which was first opened by Sir Garrard Tyrwhitt-Drake in November 1946.

The Old College, Maidstone.

The College of Priests (All Saints') was founded by Archbishop Courtenay in 1395 for the Master and twenty-four chaplains and clerks, but some of the existing building is older. The property passed to the Crown in 1537 and in 1549 George Brooke, Lord Cobham, purchased the College and its domains for £1,082. After many other changes of ownership the College property passed to Sir Robert Marsham, Bart. and the Earl of Romney, his descendant. At the turn of the century the College was used as a Church of England Middle Class School for Boys, of which Mr J. McCabe was headmaster and the lands appertaining to it were let by Lord Romney for farming purposes. Unfortunately no known illustration of the whole College has survived. This postcard, photographed from the riverside eighty years ago, shows the Gateway Tower (opposite the Church), the remains of the Cloisters (the Refectory and Kitchen with chaplains rooms above) and the River Tower which has an undercroft with a conduit to the Medway.

The only other buildings anywhere near their original condition were the Master's Tower and Master's House, shown here about 1910. The Master's Tower, with blocked arches, was probably the entrance gate in the river wall which communicated with the bridge over the Medway to the Archbishop's Park, now known as Lock Meadow. In 1949 Sir Garrard Tyrwhitt-Drake purchased the College Estate and presented it to the town. Since restoration in 1956, the Master's House has been occupied by the Kent Music School.

This postcard shows the remains of the south gatehouse of the College which has carriage and footway arches similar to those of the main entrance. Before College Road was built these arches formed the main roadway ending at the perimeter of the Estate near the present day almshouses. Other parts of the conventional College are missing, namely the Chapter House and Library; either they were never built or have disappeared. It is possible that the 'Archbishop's Precincts' were fortified in the early days as some 150 years ago excavations in the vicinity disclosed foundations of massive medieval walls.

College Farm and Hop Gardens adjoined the College Estate and were farmed during the last century by Philip Corrall, one time Mayor of Maidstone. College Road was completed in 1863 and is now one of Maidstone's principal thoroughfares. This view of College Road, shortly after it was opened, shows College Farm, the College buildings, All Saints' Church and All Saints' School on the right. College Farm survived until the 1920s.

There were two mills situated on the River Len in Mill Street (formerly Mill Lane) before the widening of the street in 1903. This mill, probably in existence since the time of Archbishop Courtenay, was sited over the existing mill race at the junction of Mill Street and Bishop's Way. The 13th-14th century Gatehouse (now the Tourist Information Office) at the main entrance to the Archbishop's Palace, was probably a former mill-house. This postcard shows the ruinous mill just before it was demolished. The mill grounds were incorporated in the 'new' Palace Gardens that were opened in July 1904.

The other mill was situated at what now is the junction of Palace Avenue and Mill Street. This view, looking along the River Len Pond from Mill Street in 1860, shows the old mill buildings and the then new Free Church in King Street. The church, replacing a former Baptist meeting house, was erected on the site of the 18th century King Street Prison. The church was demolished in the 1970s to make way for the Stoneborough Centre.

The Archbishop's Dungeon or Prison lies between All Saints' Church and the Archbishop's Palace and appears to have been part of the Priest's house given by the Rector, William of Cornhill, to the Archbishop in 1207. The Dungeon is Norman with Norman vaults and contains a 14th century undercroft. In an extension to the eastern wall is a late medieval doorway which leads to the Church.

Maidstone had two other prisons at a very early period, both situated in the High Street. The Town Prison, known as Brambles and owned by the Corporation after 1549, was part of a Town House adjacent to the Lower Court House (the former Town Hall). In 1762 the Lower Court House and Prison were demolished and the present Town Hall was built on the site. The old Brambles was transferred to an upper room of the Town Hall, the oaken walls of which, bearing the prisoners' graffiti, can be seen today. One of the prisoners, Davis, has left his record in bold Roman letters. This photograph shows one of his carvings which reads:— 'Filthy Woman is like a chain of gold tied round a swine's neck'. Other inscriptions read:— 'John Davis three times here to please his wife' and again 'Job wept at misfortune, Davis smiles, Davis 1799. 3 months'.

The original County Prison was situated in the High Street between Rose Yard and the lower end of Week Street and was purchased by the western division of Kent in 1646. It was described by William Newton in 1741 as 'an ancient stone building, inconveniently placed in the middle of the town, with no airing yard'. It was demolished in 1746 when the prisoners were transferred to a new County Prison in King Street. This postcard is a reproduction of the water colour of Maidstone High Street by G.S. Shepherd, exhibited at the Royal Academy in 1829. The original is in Maidstone Museum. The two houses on the right of the picture, opposite Rose Yard and isolated by the pavement, were pulled down in 1839. Prior to 1746 the gabled house was contiguous to the original County Prison and was the Gaoler's House. The other house was comparatively modern, having been built on part of the site of the Prison after its demolition.

Although the King Street Prison was enlarged in 1776 it had become seriously overcrowded by 1806 and a decision was taken to build larger premises at the top of Week Street. The new prison, designed by Daniel Asher Alexander and John Whichcord Sen., was opened in March 1819 taking all the prisoners from the former County Prison and the Town Prison. This postcard shows Maidstone Prison, Week Street, photographed from the air about 1930.

Among the many later owners of Chillington House were Robert South-gate, who, in 1698, used the premises for a cider making business, and William Charles, who, in 1801, carried on a felt and blanket cleaning business on the premises in conjunction with the fulling mill at Sandling. In 1840 the cleaning business was sold and William's second son, Thomas, an eccentric physician turned antiquary, inherited the property. When he died in 1855 he bequeathed over 100 fine art objects to the town thus forming the starting point of the Maidstone Museum collection. The Corporation subsequently purchased the house and adjoining garden. This early photograph of Chillington House and garden, taken from the north, shows the barn-like building at the end of the Long Gallery and Cloister that was demolished in 1873 to accommodate the present chapel. The foreground is now part of Brenchley Gardens.

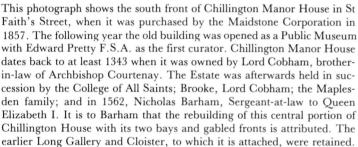

This photograph shows the south front of Chillington Manor House in St Faith's Street, when it was purchased by the Maidstone Corporation in 1857. The following year the old building was opened as a Public Museum with Edward Pretty F.S.A. as the first curator. Chillington Manor House dates back to at least 1343 when it was owned by Lord Cobham, brother-in-law of Archbishop Courtenay. The Estate was afterwards held in succession by the College of All Saints; Brooke, Lord Cobham; the Maplesden family; and in 1562, Nicholas Barham, Sergeant-at-law to Queen Elizabeth I. It is to Barham that the rebuilding of this central portion of Chillington House with its two bays and gabled fronts is attributed. The earlier Long Gallery and Cloister, to which it is attached, were retained.

Various additions and alterations have since been made to the museum. The original east wing of Chillington House, which had been degraded to a coal and straw store, was purchased in 1868 and the former west wing, which had been occupied as a separate tenement, was acquired in 1870. This rear view of Maidstone Museum photographed in the early 1870s shows the Long Gallery before the weather boarding was removed and the Observatory erected,

In 1874 Court Lodge at East Farleigh was taken down and the half-timber wing with a fine example of a kingpost, was carefully dismantled and re-erected as an annexe on the east side of the Long Gallery and Cloister. This postcard shows Court Lodge, East Farleigh, just prior to demolition.

The south front of the Museum was also restored in 1874 and iron railings, gates and forecourt pavement were added. In 1878 the tall building, which towers above the Long Gallery, known as the Observatory or Museum's Folly, was built, and in 1890 the Bentliff Art Gallery was erected at the eastern end. A Science and Art School, forming an adjunct to the Museum on the west side, was erected in 1894. (In 1968 the College transferred to Oakwood and was succeeded by Maidstone Adult Education Centre). Another addition was effected in 1897/99 by the erection of the Victoria Library and County Room, funded mainly by public subscription, in commemoration of the Diamond Jubilee of Queen Victoria. This photograph shows the formal opening of the Victoria Library and County Room which was conducted by the Lord Mayor of London on 23rd June 1899.

This postcard shows the newly restored Museum in 1900. Since that time other additions and renovations have been made including the Bearsted Wing in 1923/4 and the recent restoration programme after the 1977 fire.

THE MUSEUM AND ART GALLERY MAIDSTONE

St Faith's Church was designed by E.W. Stephens, a local architect, and erected to the east of the Museum in 1871. The Church was built on the site of St Faith's Mission, a temporary iron building, which had been erected in 1862 on the site of the 13th century chapel of St Faith demolished four years earlier. The old chapel had been converted into a ladies boarding school in the early 1800s and just prior to demolition had been a storehouse for the West Kent Militia. Original pillars of St Faith's Chapel can be seen in the Museum Gardens.

The new church of St Faith was consecrated by Archbishop Tait in September 1872. The following year Julius Brenchley, son of John Brenchley of the Lower Brewery, purchased land on the north side of the Church and Museum and, after clearing away what was at that time one of the worst slums in Maidstone, laid out public gardens which he presented to the town. The church tower, with its four stone pinnacles and three 5ft clock dials, was added in 1881.

One of two historical landmarks from Stone Street which have been preserved in Brenchley Gardens, this conduit head was one of seventeen erected in the town in 1819 for the supply of water.

This wrought iron-work construction, which decorated the top of the Lower Brewery for many years, was salvaged, when the brewery was demolished in 1970 and erected over the wishing well at the entrance to Brenchley Gardens. The six almshouses in St Faith's Street, behind the wishing well, were erected in 1700 for six poor parishioners of Maidstone, from funds left by Sir John Banks of the Friars, Aylesford and Great Buckland.

In 1874 Sir Joseph William Bazalgette, the engineer of the Thames embankment and the London Sewers, was asked to draw up plans for a new bridge at Maidstone as the medieval structure had been declared unsafe. This photograph shows the ancient bridge and College Lock, taken from the tumbling bay of the lock in the summer of 1877.

On 24th October 1877 the first pile of the new bridge was driven on a new site a few inches north of the old one. Twenty-two months later the new Maidstone Bridge of three arches, with a waterway 149ft wide, 32ft wider than its predecessor and costing over £55,000, stood ready for the opening. This photograph shows the medieval bridge and the present bridge under construction in 1879.

The afternoon of 6th August 1879 was declared a public holiday and crowds of people attended the opening ceremony. Bunting and coloured lights bedecked the High Street and an ornate archway had been erected at the eastern approach to the bridge. At 2 p.m. a procession arrived from the Town Hall and after the customary speeches the Mayor, Alderman Charles Ellis, was handed a bottle of curiosities. The bottle contained: a commemoration medal of the opening of the bridge; photographs of the Mayor and Corporation; a copy of the Times; the local newspapers; telegrams from abroad and coins bearing the head of Queen Victoria. This photograph, looking along Fair Meadow, shows the crowds of people at the ceremony. (Note the old Town Wharf and the row of elm trees which were planted after the storm in August 1763 when a previous row of elms was destroyed).

The Mayor placed the bottle under the topmost stone of the bridge and cutting the tape, declared the bridge open. As he did so, thousands of spectators cheered, salvoes of artillery were fired in Fair Meadow, a fountain played on the Medway, the church bells rang and the band of the Royal Engineers played the National Anthem. After the ceremony 5,000 school children marched to Mote Park where they had tea and were presented with commemoration medals. Later that evening a grand firework display was presented by Brock's of Crystal Palace; one of the set pieces bore the inscription 'Success to the New Bridge'. For a few months the two bridges stood side by side until eventually the ancient bridge was demolished and the stone removed in lighters to Burham, where it was used in the erection of cottages.

ALLINGTON LOCK, NEAR MAIDSTONE.

The Medway became navigable via locks between Maidstone and Tonbridge from 1739, and in 1792 the Lower Medway Navigation Company constructed this important lock at Allington where formerly there had only been a ford. Allington Lock, 2½ miles north of Maidstone, became the last point on the River Medway to be tidal. College Lock at Maidstone was dismantled in 1882, the remains of which can still be seen opposite Lock Meadow near All Saints' Church.

Floods had always been a threat to Maidstone. To lessen the problem new tidal sluices, costing £18,000, were opened at Allington on Wednesday 4th August 1937 by the Minister of Agriculture, Mr W.S. Morrison. Allington Locks, being the last locks controlling the level of the river before it reached the sea, were therefore in the key position as regards land drainage of the whole catchment area of the Medway. As an added protection a £3,000,000 flood barrier, near Tonbridge, came into operation in 1981.

This derelict, ivy-clad castle on the southern bank of the Medway, near Allington Locks, was purchased in 1905 by Lord Martin Conway and his American wife Katrina from Lord Romney for £4,800. The castle, originally built in 1282 by Stephen of Penchester and added to by the Wyatts, had fallen into decay after a disastrous fire in the 17th century. Lord Conway set about restoring the ruin to its former condition using it for a place to live and to house his vast collection of art treasures. Following the death of Lord Conway in 1937, Allington Castle passed to his daughter Agnes Horsfield who let the property to Mr Alfred C. Bossom M.P. and his wife.

This postcard shows Mr and Mrs Bossom in the grounds of the restored castle in 1937. When Agnes died in 1951 the Castle was sold to the Carmelite Order from Aylesford Priory, for the sum of £15,000, and the family possessions were auctioned in the Great Hall at Allington.

Vinters, another of Maidstone's historic mansions, was named after the family of Vinter to whom it belonged in the 14th century. After many changes of ownership the house was purchased in 1783 by James Whatman, the famous paper-maker from Turkey Mill. He modernised and enlarged the mansion and landscaped the parkland. In 1852 the house was further enlarged and a Jacobean frontage was added to Roger Vinter's original house. Members of the Whatman family continued to live at Vinters until 1950 when Miss Louisa Whatman died there at the age of 92. Vinters Estate was sold to the Kent County Council in 1952 and the mansion was demolished. It is still possible to see the old ice house and the ornamental lake; the ha-ha is a listed feature. In recent years houses, a crematorium and TV South Studios have been built on parts of the Estate. The rest of the parkland is soon to be opened as a Country Park.

Springfield, one of the first paper mills in the country to be powered by steam, was opened in January 1807 by William Balston, a former apprentice to James Whatman at Turkey Mill. Six generations of the Balston family managed Springfield Mill until the early 1970s when the firm of W. & R. Balston merged with H. Reeve Angel to form the public company Whatman Reeve Angel, now one of the county's largest exporters of specialist papers. This photograph was taken inside Springfield Mill about 1906.

SPRINGFIELD MAIDSTONE. Y&C 572

Springfield House, situated on the east bank of the Medway between Springfield and Medway Mills, was built in 1891 by Alfred Waterhouse for R.J. Balston, the grandson of William Balston. The house took the place of an older residence of the same name and was where most of the Balstons first saw the light of day. In July 1907 the centenary celebrations of Springfield Mill were conducted in the grounds of the house. Springfield House is now owned and occupied by Kent County Council.

In October 1820 William Gosling, a gas contractor, purchased a piece of ground between St Peter's Street and the Medway and erected a Gas Works with one gasometer. A year later, on 27th September 1821, Maidstone was, for the first time, illuminated by gas. 'It had a most brilliant appearance from the disposition of the lamp columns in the High Street and conferred infinite credit on Mr Gosling, the contractor.' This postcard shows Maidstone High Street in the 1890s when it was gaslit.

In 1823 William Gosling sold his gasworks to thirty local businessmen who formed the Maidstone Gas Light & Coke Co. Another gasometer was added in 1835 and in 1844 Gosling's original gas holder was replaced. Gas cooking apparatus was first supplied to private consumers in 1851 and in 1858 another gasometer was ordered. That same year the Company was renamed the Maidstone Gas Company. Subsequently the property on the other side of St Peter's Street was purchased and two large holders were erected, one in 1872 and the other in 1901. This postcard, dated 1914, shows three gasometers on the St Peter's site.

Throughout the early years of this century Maidstone linked up with several other small gas works in the area and in May 1949 the Maidstone Gas Company became part of the South Eastern Gas Board. When Natural Gas was found in sufficient quantities in the 1960s to supply all of Britain, the days of manufactured gas were numbered. Maidstone Gas Works closed down leaving one gas holder for reserves and the Segas offices.

In 1901 Maidstone's Electricity Works were built in Fair Meadow adjoining the Public Baths, at the northern end of the Cattle Market. The buildings and shaft were designed and constructed under the supervision of Mr T.F. Bunting, the Borough Surveyor, and the builders were G.E.Wallis & Sons, Maidstone. The electrical engineers were Stevens and Barker who employed about 30 men and boys at Maidstone on electrical installation work. (A few years later W.A. Stevens went into partnership with Thomas Tilling and the firm was renamed Tilling-Stevens).

The Electricity Works chimney was built larger than necessary as it was originally intended to accommodate a refuse destructor. It was 152ft high and was built from the outside using no less than 1,000 poles for the scaffolding. It took 7½ months to erect and cost £1,873. When the Electricity Works opened there were 225 consumers connected to the supply, most of them for lighting only. The plant was run from 3 p.m. till 11.30 p.m. and a storage battery was used, if necessary, for the rest of the time. Six men were employed at the Works and six men were on meters and house wiring. By the end of the first year there was a deficit of £3,000 but all this changed in ensuing years. In 1919/20 the system of generation changed from Direct Current (D.C.) to Alternating Current (A.C.). The Electricity Works closed on 24th March 1967 and the buildings were subsequently sold to the Maidstone Borough Council and were later demolished to make way for the new road system and St Peter's Bridge.

A photograph taken outside Maidstone Museum, of the Corporation, when the Electricity Works were opened on 19th December 1901. The Mayor, Alderman W. Brownscombe, is in the centre of the front row, with the Deputy Mayor, Councillor Edmund Vaughan, Chairman of the Electric Lighting Committee, on his right, and Councillor William Morling, who had introduced the scheme of electrification, on his left.

14

Maidstone Borough Police Force, who served under the Watch Committee of the Town Council, began duty in 1836. The original force consisted of the Superintendent, Mr Thomas Fancett, two inspectors, Mr George Brown and Mr John Sharp, and a corps of fourteen men. All these men were ordered to wear whiskers; the 'relief of the order not to shave' was not granted until 1873. The police station was in King Street, (nearly opposite the entrance to Church Street) and was in use until 1908 when larger premises were built in Palace Avenue.

The Maidstone Borough Police Force outside king Street Police Station in 1906. Mr A.C. Mackintosh, in the middle of the front row, was appointed the first Chief Constable in 1895 and remained in command until 1921.

The 'new' Maidstone Police Station, in Palace Avenue, was built of Kentish Ragstone from designs by Ruck & Smith and cost about £9,500 in 1908. The Station contained eight cells and a complete range of departmental offices with assembly and recreation rooms for men. There were also quarters for a married constable and an adjoining residence for the Chief Constable. A public mortuary was also erected on the site. These premises are still in use and have recently been enlarged and modernised.

The Maidstone Borough Police Force outside Palace Avenue Police Station in 1914. In 1921 steps were taken for the merging of the Borough Force with that of the Kent County Constabulary. Negotiations failed however and Maidstone Police Force remained independent until the compulsory amalgamation with the County Constabulary in April 1943.

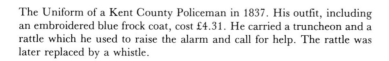

The Kent County Constabulary was established in 1857 and Wren's Cross, a house on the junction of Stone Street, Mote Road and Knightrider Street was taken over for use as Police Headquarters. Captain Ruxton, a former army officer, was appointed Chief Constable and he stayed in command for 37 years. When he retired in 1894, at 77 years of age, he had out-served every member of the force, as all the original 222 had either died, retired or left for other appointments. The Kent County Constabulary moved to the present headquarters in Sutton Road in April 1940.

The Uniform of a Kent County Policeman in 1837. His outfit, including an embroidered blue frock coat, cost £4.31. He carried a truncheon and a rattle which he used to raise the alarm and call for help. The rattle was later replaced by a whistle.

Maidstone's first organised fire service was provided by the Kent Insurance Company (Kent Fire Office) between 1804 and 1901. The Company owned two manual fire engines and enrolled men to attend the fires. This photograph shows their new Merryweather manual fire engine, purchased in 1883, in the 'Kent' fire engine house situated beside the Company's office in the High Street. On the wall behind the firemen can be seen the Company's 'Invicta' horse emblem, a somewhat dilapidated example of which still exists on a building in Rose Yard.

Another view of the Merryweather photographed outside the Kent Fire Office in the High Street. The horses were usually 'borrowed' for a fee from the local cab rank.

In 1900 three stalls, at the southern end of Market Buildings, were converted into a fire station by Maidstone Corporation and in 1901 the Maidstone Borough Fire Brigade was founded taking over from the 'Kent' and a Volunteer Fire Brigade which had been supported by the Corporation since 1873. The new Borough Brigade also inherited the 'Kent's' two manual fire engines, the Merryweather and a Shand Mason purchased in 1886. Captain Gates, of the Kent Fire Office Brigade, became Captain of the Borough Brigade. Captain Gates is in the middle of the front row in this postcard of the Borough Brigade photographed in the early 1900s.

The Borough Brigade also purchased a Shand Mason steam fire engine in 1901, named 'The Queen'. This postcard shows 'The Queen' at the fire at Snodland Paper Mill on 12th August 1906. It was at this fire that Captain Gates was highly commended for his efforts. 'The Queen' was in service until the Second World War by which time three Dennis fire engines had been purchased, 'Ethel' in 1914, 'Invicta' in 1928 and 'Vanguard' in 1939. In 1941 Maidstone Fire Brigade became part of the National Fire Service and in 1958 a new fire station was opened in Loose Road. The old fire station in Market Buildings closed in 1967.

The Medway was for centuries the town's main means of transport and by 1834 more than fifty barges were trading from Maidstone. Hops, paper, fruit, cloth, corn, leather and wool were among the many commodities transported to London. This postcard shows the barges 'Verona' and 'Three Brothers' and the tug 'Ranger' passing through the locks at Allington in the early years of this century.

In the 19th century many of the town's industries were situated along the river, served by several wharves. Rail, and later road transport, gradually took most of the freight traffic and by the 1920s the river trade had begun to decline, as had the need for the riverside position of the factories and warehouses. This postcard shows Bridge Wharf on the far side of Maidstone Bridge and, on the nearer side, the landing stage by Town Wharf. Bridge Wharf and the adjoining buildings were demolished prior to the construction of Bishop's Way.

The South Eastern Railway was the first train service to reach Maidstone by a branch line from Paddock Wood on 25th September 1844 and the station was built near the far end of Hart Street. The line was extended north from Maidstone to Strood on 18th June 1856 and the present Maidstone West Station was built and the station of 1844 closed. Maidstone East Station did not come into operation until 1st June 1874 when the London, Chatham & Dover Railway extended the line from Otford to Maidstone. This postcard shows the station site and the building of the L.C.D.R. at Maidstone. In the background are the Victoria Hotel and the Sessions House now obscured by the Kent County Council Offices. The line was double tracked in 1881 and three years later extended to Ashford.

Horse-drawn vehicles for passenger transport were still in operation in Maidstone in the early 1900's. These two 'Ongley' horse buses, at the Three Squirrels Public House at Stockbury, were on the service route between Maidstone and Sittingbourne.

Maidstone's first municipal transport commenced in 1904 when the Corporation opened a tramway between the High Street and the Fountain Inn, Barming. This postcard shows tram No. 3, shortly after the opening, on the outward journey to Barming along the Tonbridge Road.

The tramway was extended to Loose in October 1907 and to Tovil in January 1908. This postcard shows the tram rails being laid at Tovil just prior to opening. The Tovil tramway was not as successful as the Barming and Loose services so a one-man operated demi-car was introduced in 1909 in place of the conventional tramcars. After the First World War, with an upsurge in labour at the Tovil Paper Mills, the original trams were reinstated.

The Barming trams were replaced by eight Ransome trolleybuses on 1st May 1928. This postcard shows one of these early trolleybuses at the top of the High Street. The Loose route was converted to trolleybuses in 1930 and the Tovil route was replaced by motorbuses in 1929. Trolleybuses continued in operation in Maidstone until 1967 when they were phased out in favour of motorbuses.

High Street, Maidstone. 2070.

Maidstone Bridge.

Another of the early Maidstone Fleet of Ransomes crossing Maidstone Bridge. The motorbus alongside was built by the local firm Tilling-Stevens and operated on the London Road service.

The first London Road bus service ran from Penenden Heath to Queens Avenue in 1924 but owing to the rapid development of housing estates along the London Road, the terminus was moved to Buckland Lane in 1927, Palmar Road by 1933, Grace Avenue in 1937 and Allington Way in 1950. This postcard shows the arrival of the 2 o'clock London Road bus at Palmar Road during the great hailstorm on Monday 19th June 1933.

Maidstone was one of the first authorities in the country to build a public swimming bath. This engraving shows the Italianate Public Baths and Wash-houses in Fair Meadow as designed by Arthur Ashpital and John Whichcord Junior in 1851. The original bath was 48ft by 22ft and a larger bath measuring 90ft by 36ft, containing 100,000 gallons of water, was added in 1895. The buildings were demolished in 1976 to make way for the present road system and St Peter's Bridge. There was a Bathing Establishment at 68 Week Street in 1839 advertised as follows:— A Shower Bath . . . 1/-, Cold, Salt & Fresh Water Bath . . . 1/6d, Warm, Salt & Fresh Water Bath . . . 2/-, and Sulphur Bath . . . 3/6d.

Fair Day in Fair Meadow in 1897. The Pleasure Fairs, with swings, roundabouts, stalls and side shows, were held in Fair Meadow during most of the 19th century and the early years of this century, taking place on 12th May, 20th June and 17th October. On these days the High Street and parts of Week Street were lined with make-shift stalls where farmers and traders sold their produce and wares.

Market Day in Fair Meadow in the 1890s; the Public Baths can be seen in the background. The weekly stock market was held in Fair Meadow from 1826 until 1919 when it was transferred to its present site in Lock Meadow, which had been purchased by the Corporation in 1892 at a cost of £6,700. The Agricultural Hall in Lock Meadow was officially opened on 12th May (Fair Day) and a Produce and Poultry Market was inaugurated there in June 1919.

Corn, Fish, Meat and Vegetable Markets were originally held in the High Street, but moved to new market buildings, designed by John Whichcord Senior, erected between the High Street and Earl Street in 1825. The layout of these buildings, however, was unsatisfactory and the present Corn Exchange and Market Buildings were built ten years later. A Concert Hall was added in 1869, and reconstructed into the Municipal Theatre in 1955. The theatre was refurbished in 1970 and renamed the Hazlitt Theatre after the essayist and critic William Hazlitt who was born in Rose Yard. William's father was minister at the Unitarian Nonconformist Church (on the right of the photograph) from 1770-1780. The Church, dating from 1736, still has its original pulpit and gallery. The Market Buildings Complex is shortly to be redeveloped.

This device, erected at the High Street entrance of Market Buildings, was used as a sack rest by customers leaving the Corn Exchange with their heavy sacks of corn. It has only recently been removed.

The West Kent Infirmary & Dispensary, built in Marsham Street in 1832, was also designed by John Whichcord Senior. When first opened the building was lit by candles and drinking water came from a well in the grounds. The establishment became known as the West Kent General Hospital in 1862 and has since been enlarged several times. In 1982 the West Kent Hospital was superseded by the new Maidstone General Hospital in Hermitage Lane and the old building is undergoing demolition. This postcard shows the West Kent General Hospital in 1909.

The Howard de Walden Institute for Women was built in Marsham Street in 1891 by the liberality of the Dowager Lady Howard de Walden of Mote House. Classes for cookery, dressmaking, nursing, drawing, singing, French and Bible Study were held there when it was first opened. During the typhoid epidemic in 1897 many of the nurses who came to Maidstone from the London hospitals to tend the sick were accommodated in the building. This postcard shows the Institute when it was a V.A.D. hospital during the First World War. Afterwards the building was purchased by the West Kent Hospital for a Nurses Home. The building now houses the Maidstone Community Support Centre.

Marsham Street looking towards Queen Anne Road in 1907. The West Kent General Hospital is on the far left and the Howard de Walden Institute is the tall building on the opposite side of the road. The small steeple, above the houses in Queen Anne Road, is on the top of the old Maidstone Grammar School for Girls in Albion Place. The school, which now supplies sixth form accommodation for Maidstone's Invicta Grammar School for Girls, is shortly to be demolished to make way for a new Maidstone Road Scheme linking the A249 and A229 via the A20. Marsham Street was the first target in Maidstone to be bombed in the Second World War. Two bombs fell between the Hospital and the Nurses Home, killing two women sheltering in a basement.

Barming Asylum, Maidstone.

Following the purchase of thirty-seven acres of land at Barming Heath, Barming Asylum, costing £50,000, with accommodation for 174 patients, was opened on 1st January 1833 and was considered to be one of the most modern asylums of its kind. Designed by John Whichcord Senior, the building, like other mental homes in the country, was modelled on prison lines. One of the first patients to be admitted to the new Asylum was John Nichols Thom who was convinced that he was Sir William Percy Honeywood Courtenay, the new Messiah. He was released in the autumn of 1837 through the influence of his wife, and in the following May organised a riot against the King's troops in Bossenden Wood, Dunkirk. Thom and eight of his followers were killed and Lieutenant Henry Boswell Bennett in the 45th Regiment and two of his soldiers also lost their lives.

In 1850 a chronic asylum, with accommodation for 200 persons, was added, and in 1864 (the beginning of what is described as the 'era of chemical restraint', which gradually superseded mechanical restraint), the authorities acquired a further 112 acres on the west side of the Estate and built a third asylum between 1867 and 1872. In later years such patients as were able either worked on the adjoining farms or helped in the kitchen or laundry. This photograph shows the laundry room at the Asylum in 1904.

The kitchen at the Asylum also photographed in 1904. A further enlargement took place in 1906 with the addition of two blocks for 100 patients each, and another addition in 1912 when the 'era of hospitalisation' began. Barming Asylum, which was virtually a prison in the early days, became the Kent County Mental Hospital and again in later years Oakwood Hospital. Even the address was altered from Asylum Road to St Andrew's Road. In 1982 the new Maidstone General Hospital was built on the northern end of the site.

A new Nurses Home and Training School, for the Kent County Mental Hospital, was opened in Hermitage Lane by the Queen's Aunt, Princess Mary, Viscountess Lascelles, on 7th June 1927. The Princess was received by the Lord Lieutenant of Kent, the Marquis Camden, who presented to her Sir Henry Leonard, Bart., Chairman of the Committee of the Hospital. Along the path some 60 nurses formed the guard of honour.

On arrival at the Home, more than 2,000 people flocked to see the Princess as she was presented with a bouquet of flowers. After the formal opening and speeches, Her Royal Highness inspected the new premises and, crossing the road, walked into the Hospital grounds and visited the main buildings.

Escorted by Dr Wolseley Lewis, the Medical Superintendent, and the Matron, Princess Mary was conducted through the Infirmary, the Acute and Convalescent Wards, the Solaria and the Operating Theatre. Returning to the Home for tea, she passed through the final and most imposing guard of honour, 800 Girl Guides and Brownies.

The Maidstone Union Workhouse at Coxheath, 4 miles from Maidstone, was opened in March 1838 to take all the poor from Maidstone and the surrounding parishes. There were special wards for casual paupers who were called upon to do certain tasks in return for a night's board and lodging. A chapel was built in the Union Grounds in 1844 and Maidstone Workhouse Schools were built in East Farleigh in 1857. When this postcard was produced in 1916 there were 303 inmates at the Union Workhouse and 127 children in the Workhouse Schools. In the 1930s Maidstone Union Workhouse became the Maidstone & District Public Assistance Institution. Later it was absorbed into the National Health Service and became Linton Hospital, caring mainly for the elderly. During the 18th century Coxheath was the site of a large military camp and two relics of the old military occupation have remained; the Barrack Square, which was incorporated in the grounds of the Workhouse, and Clock House, an 18th century residence which is said to have been the military headquarters and officers' mess. Coxheath, formerly a sprawling hamlet on waste and common land and reputed to be the haunt of highwaymen and robbers, only became a civil parish in 1964, portions being taken of the adjoining parishes of Linton, Loose and East Farleigh.

East Maidstone also had a Pest House. This old house stood at the junction of College Road and Tovil Road and was demolished in 1926.

These two cottages in Bower Lane, at the top of the hill leading to Tovil's former Railway Station, were originally West Maidstone's Pest House where persons suffering from contagious diseases were detained.

Tonbridge Road in 1910, showing Westborough Congregational Church (demolished in 1977) with Bower Lane off to the right and Bower Street to the left. This area of Maidstone used to be called 'The Bower', taking its name from a field called Bower Down in the time of Henry VIII. Warwick House, behind the iron railings on the far corner of Bower Street on the Tonbridge Road, was the original Bower House and for many years belonged to the Corpus Christi Guild in Earl Street.

Congregational Church, Tonbridge Road, Maidstone.

Bower Farmhouse, a half-timbered property, was situated at the junction of Bower Lane and Tonbridge Road. The Farmhouse was demolished about 1872 and Westborough Congregational Church was built in 1876 on the site of the former farm buildings on the corner of Bower Place and Tonbridge Road.

Bower Street as it appeared eighty years ago with not a vehicle in sight, apart from the local delivery cart which brought bread, buns, pastries, cake and milk to the door. There were also several small shops in the Street including Howlett's General Store and Off-licence at No. 16, and George Planden's Bakery and General Store at Nos 77 and 79. Note the baker's boy and the horse posing for the camera.

BOWER STREET, MAIDSTONE.—46.

This postcard, photographed in 1906, shows Old Tovil Road, looking towards Upper Stone Street from Rawdon Road. Arthur Briggs kept the General Shop on the corner and William Goodbody was the proprietor of the Fortune of War Public House on the Stone Street corner. The spire, behind the houses, belongs to St Philip's Church on the Kingsley Estate.

A horse and cart waits outside the Old English Gentleman Public House in Church Street, Tovil, in 1907. Next door is Timothy Oddy's butcher's shop and further down is William Hood's, the newsagents. The Old English Gentleman closed in 1916. Tovil, a hamlet and ecclesiastical parish, formed in February 1843 from the civil parishes of Maidstone, East Farleigh and Loose, is about one mile south of Maidstone on the banks of the Medway, and is now within the Municipal Borough. St Stephen's Church, Tovil, consecrated in 1841, is now redundant.

In 1886 the South Eastern Railway Company constructed an iron bridge over the Medway which carried a short branch line to a goods station at Tovil. In the early days the line was busy transporting paper from Tovil Mills but road transport took over and later the paper-mills declined and the goods station was closed in the 1970s. The railbridge was demolished in 1986 but the iron bridge for foot passengers, erected in 1872, has survived.

Great Buckland House, a fine Tudor mansion lying between the London Road and the Medway in West Maidstone, was demolished prior to the building of Maidstone Girls' Grammar School on the site in 1938. The Buckland Estate dated back to the 13th century and in 1270 was owned by Walter de Bocland. The Estate later passed to the College of All Saints and was subsequently granted to George Brooke, Lord Cobham, whose grandson forfeited the property for treason. The Estate next passed to Robert, Earl of Salisbury, whose descendent William, in 1618, broke up Buckland into three portions, Great Buckland, Little Buckland and South Buckland. Great Buckland was purchased by Lawrence Washington's son-in-law, William Horsepoole, and was later sold to Sir John Banks Bart. from whom it descended to the Earl of Aylesford. The rest of the Buckland Estate passed to Lord Romney.

Buckland Hill was one of the first roads to be developed to the south-east of the Estate. This postcard, photographed in the early 1900s, shows the footpath to the High Level Bridge, The Medway Milling Company, The Sessions House, Maidstone Prison and, on the far right, the tower of St Francis' Church. The steeple of St Paul's Church may be seen in the trees on the left.

This postcard of London Road, and the next of Palmar Road, show some of the first houses on the Little Buckland Estate, built by Cox Brothers in the late 1920s.

London Road, Little Buckland Estate, Maidstone.

Two of the roads on this housing development are named after the original Buckland Estate, namely Buckland Lane and Little Buckland Avenue. Little Buckland Farm Cottage still exists and can be seen near the railway arch at the bottom of Buckland Lane. The Cottage, dating from the 14th century, is one of Maidstone's oldest properties and is a listed building.

Somerfield Terrace, London Road, in 1907. These prosperous houses, built at the beginning of the 19th century, were specially erected for the officers of the Cavalry at the Barracks in Sandling Road. In recent years several of these houses have been converted into a private hospital. The Toll House was sited just beyond these houses, on the London Road, in the 19th century.

This old house inscribed 'IBM 1672' was removed from Pudding Lane in the early 19th century and rebuilt at 2 & 3 Bedford Place, London Road. The house now belongs to the Maidstone Borough Council and is the local Planning Office.

A view of Earl Street looking towards Week Street in 1908. Note the large knife outside the Mid Kent Grinding Works & Cutlers Shop at 12 Earl Street and the ancient Roebuck Inn on the corner at 2 Earl Street. Cruttendens and the adjoining shop in Week Street have now made way for the present Marks & Spencer Store. Earl Street was called Earl's Lane in 1599 and was later renamed Bullock Lane, having for many years been the locality of Maidstone's stockmarket before it was transferred to Fair Meadow in 1826.

Another view of Earl Street, looking towards the Medway, in the early 1920s. Of interest are:— St Faith's Parish Room and Earl Street Garage (Mongers) immediately behind the cars; Rodney Wharf (Pine & Sons) in Fair Meadow; Fremlin's Brewery on the north corner of Earl Street and Fair Meadow; the houses next to Fremlin's, which were demolished in the 1930s to accommodate Museum Street; and the remnants of Earl's Place which are incorporated in the building behind the small girls. The extra tall building is the Conservative Club (note the sculptured head of Disraeli over the entrance) and to the right is the Market House Public House, formerly called the Coal Barge.

This photograph, taken in the early 1930s, shows the premises of George Prentis & Sons, Wine and Spirit Merchants, at 37 Earl Street, on the corner of Pudding Lane. The name of Prentis was connected with this business from 1716 until it was taken over by Fremlin's in 1960. The premises, although rebuilt in 1885, still retained early vaults dating from 1764. One alley in the cellarage was 140ft long and contained 72 bins averaging 50 dozen bottles in each. George Prentis & Sons also had a shop at 1 Middle Row next to the Town Hall. Part of the Earl Street building is now used by Invicta Radio.

HIGH ST MAIDSTONE

The Lower High Street in 1908. On the left hand side are:— Wallace Brett, confectioner & fruiterer; Goulden & Wind, piano manufacturers; The General Post Office; and A.E. Wilkinson & Son, Toy & Fishing Tackle Warehouse. Of interest on the opposite side are:— Loder & Sons Motor Garage; William Weekes, engineers; The King's Head; and The Penny Bazaar. Note the mobile placard in the middle of the road and the old wharves along the riverside. Several of the shops on the right hand side of the High Street have recently been demolished for future development.

This busy scene in the High Street in 1912 shows No. 1 tram (with added destination box and lowered headlamp), on the outward journey to Barming. Carriers carts are lined up in the centre of the road while their horses are cared for at the stables of either the Queen's Head or the Rose and Crown.

HIGH STREET SHOWING STAR HOTEL, MAIDSTONE

A 1920s postcard looking towards the top of the High Street. The small van on the right hand side is parked outside W.H. Cutbush's Butcher's Shop at No. 4 Middle Row. On the other side are:— The Royal Star Hotel; International Stores; Macfisheries Ltd; Jackson & Smith (confectioners & fruiterers); W.H. Smith & Son; and Treadwell Bros. All of these establishments have gone from the High Street, even the Royal Star, which had been the leading hostelry in the town since the 16th century, has recently succumbed to progress and become a shopping arcade.

Walter Ruck's shop at 11 High Street, Maidstone at the turn of the century. On sale were books, stationery, maps, newspapers, fancy goods and artists' materials.

Walter Ruck printed and published his own postcards and provided a circulating and subscription library. He was an agent for Norwich Union Fire and Life Insurance Societies. The shop was also the Maidstone Branch Office of the Kentish Express and Ashford News. W.H. Smith & Son took over from Walter Ruck in the 1920s.

A cab waits at the corner of the High Street and the Undercliffe, about 1890. The Undercliffe was a small thoroughfare which ran from the High Street through to the riverside, passing behind Bridge Wharf and the neighbouring riverside buildings. Bishop's Way meets the High Street on this corner today.

Denniss Paine & Co., tailors & outfitters, at 3 & 4 High Street in the 1890s. The Company also had a pawnbroker's business at 1 & 2 Rose Yard. (Note the three balls over the entrance to Rose Yard). In 1909 the London County & Westminster Bank (the present National Westminster Bank) was built on the site of the High Street premises. It is interesting to note that for many years Denniss Paine & Co. had a general drapers at 24, 25, 26 & 27 High Street (next to Pudding Lane) and an ironmongers and builders merchants at 61 High Street (next to the Queen's Head). The Company still has an ironmongers at Forstal Road, Aylesford.

A close-up of Blake & Son's Drapers Shop at 93 & 94 High Street in 1905, showing the cast iron front with tiled infilling, as designed by Arthur Ashpital and John Whichcord Junior in 1855. This shop still had an automatic cash railway up till the time it closed in the late 1970s.

Week Street, photographed from the High Street junction, in 1908. Upson & Co., boot and shoe makers, can be seen at 3 & 5 Week Street, with Lipton's at No. 7 and Morton Shoe Co. at No. 9. Next door at No. 11 is S.P. Sanders furniture shop. Further along behind the road sweeper, deliveries are being made to the Bell Hotel. The Bell Hotel closed in the 1920s, but the date 1711 (when the inn was re-fronted) has remained on the building and probably indicates the year in which the licence was transferred from the original Bell Hotel at the top of Gabriel's Hill.

The Maidstone Coffee Palace and Central Temperance Hotel, Week Street, in 1904. The Coffee Palace was hired as a store for the reception and distribution of medical appliances during the Typhoid Epidemic in 1897. During alterations a Tudor fireplace and a carved oak ceiling were revealed. In the 1920s the Misses Grant and Hickmott used the premises as an art needlework department. The Central was one of two temperance hotels in Maidstone, the other was Winterbottom's at 27 Gabriel's Hill. The Central also had private apartments at 17 Brewer Street.

View of the Central Hotel from the rear gardens. Littlewoods Store is now on the site of the Coffee Palace and Central Hotel.

Edith Cavell, the nurse who was shot by the Germans in Brussels in 1915, was a young probationer in Maidstone during the typhoid epidemic and worked in the temporary hospital at Padsole School. She, with five other nursing companions from the London Hospital, lodged at the home of Mrs Josiah Baker at 72 Bank Street. Nurse Cavell, along with one hundred other nurses, received a silver medal for her services from the Mayor of Maidstone on 8th December 1897. The presentation was in the Bentliff Gallery at the Maidstone Museum and was attended by the Lord Mayor of London.

G. Verrall
and Sons.

Corn, Seed,
Cake,
Hay & Straw
Merchants.

HART STREET,

MAIDSTONE.

George Verrall & Sons' premises at 13 Hart Street in 1903. Crittenden's shoe repairers were next door at No. 11 and Robert Batcheller & Sons Ltd, timber merchants, were at No. 15. All these buildings were demolished prior to the erection of the Law Courts near this site, which were opened by Her Majesty Queen Elizabeth II on 31st October 1984. This postcard was published by the London Photographic Company whose studios were at Broadway House, near the Bridge, and whose works were at 24 Melville Road, Maidstone.

The New Inn and public toilets at the top of Week Street in 1908. The New Inn dated back to 1860 and when the railway came to East Maidstone in 1874 the establishment became known as the New Inn & Railway Hotel. The Hotel contained the largest assembly room in Maidstone and provided accommodation for public meetings and concerts. After the Second World War the Hotel was renamed the Wig & Gown. The building has recently been demolished and the modern construction of the Municipal Mutual Insurance Co. is now on the site.

The Running Horse Inn at Sandling, Maidstone, was advertised in 1906 as follows:— 'The fully licensed Running Horse at Sandling, on the High Road to Rochester and Chatham, and at the junction roads from Aylesford and Boxley, is a favourite resort; the attraction of which is enhanced by a tea garden about 80 yards square. Cold luncheons and refreshments of all kinds are served at moderate charges. The Inn is within a few minutes walk of Allington, Allington Lock and Boxley Abbey. Proprietor — J. Harrod.' In 1938 a new Running Horse, in mock Tudor style with a Norfolk reed thatch, was built on the site. The Public House was modernised again in 1987 and is now a 'Harvester' Steak House.

Lyle's Hop Ale Brewery, East Layne House, 91 King Street, in 1901. (King Street was called East Layne before 1799.) Daniel T.J. Lyle founded these mineral water works at Maidstone in 1870 and by the early 1900s other factories, managed by members of his family, had opened up all over Kent. For many years a large ginger beer bottle decorated the front of the building but was removed just before the Second World War. (See Old Maidstone, Vol.1 page 12.) The Company ceased trading in 1966 and the premises are now occupied by Stonham, the chemist.

Holloway's Bakery, established in 1834, had their premises at 69 Boxley Road. This baker's cart was a familiar sight in Maidstone during the early years of this century and is seen here in front of the allotments in Albert Street, off Sandling Road.

Walter W. Bannister, motor engineer and garage proprietor, of 62 King Street, designed and built this light car in 1909. He exhibited it at an early Olympia Show and subsequently put it on the market. Bannister had received his training with Easton, Anderson and Goolden Ltd, engineers of London & Erith, and had moved to Maidstone from Crawley in 1904. His premises, then situated next to King Street Sub Post Office, had belonged to Loder & Sons, coachbuilders, and had facilities for accumulator charging and steam vulcanising. Bannister ran his own car hire and repair business, supplied commercial vehicles for heavy work and sold garage supplies including petrol. He also gave driving lessons and was sole agent for Argyll Motors for West Kent. This postcard was photographed opposite Bannister's garage, in front of the entrance to Cecil Square and J. Weekes Sports Shop (now Safeways Supermarket). (See postcard of King Street on page 15.) The business was later taken over by the motor engineers, R.S. Miles & Co.

Miss V. Bannister, Maidstone, on her "Unecar".

The Mayor of Maidstone, Councillor F.J. Oliver, and the Corporation, met the West Kent Yeomanry at Maidstone West Station on 19th July 1901, on their return from the Boer War in South Africa. This view shows the procession in the Broadway, headed by Chief Constable Mackintosh and a County Constable, on its way to a Thanksgiving Service in All Saints' church.

All the leading establishments in the town were decorated with flags, streamers etc., and a banner with the words 'Welcome to our Yeomanry' was strung across the High Street. As the contingent of men passed by the Cannon, spectators climbed on the stationary carriers' carts to get a better view. After the Church Service a banquet was held for the Yeomanry in the Corn Exchange and as it was such a hot day, Punkahs had to be used to keep the air in motion.

Princess Henry of Battenberg, daughter of Queen Victoria, visited Maidstone on Wednesday 28th May 1902 and opened a sale of work at Vinters, the residence of Mrs Whatman, where she sold dolls, pin cushions, art needlework, scent sachets and baskets of sweets from her own craft stall. Afterwards Her Royal Highness distributed medals to those members of the Maidstone Companies of the Royal Medical Corps Volunteers who had served in South Africa. The first to be presented was Sgt Weedon who had been specially promoted by Lord Kitchener for great gallantry.

The Maidstone Tannery, photographed shortly after its reconstruction in 1900. The tannery and offices covered 2 acres of ground on the north side of the Len Pond in Mill Street and was claimed to be one of the best and most completely equipped tan yards in the south of England. Mr A.M. Dorman ran the business and used only oak bark, one of the oldest and first-rate materials known to have been used for tanning.

The bark was crushed inside the tannery by machines driven by a steam engine and some of the hides stayed in the bark liquor for as long as 12 months. In addition to the tanning there was a considerable fellmongers trade giving employment to a large number of hands. This photograph was taken inside the tannery in the early years of this century.

In 1917 the Maidstone Tannery was taken over by William Rootes, a former motor dealer in Week Street and Pudding Lane, who had been demobilised from the Royal Naval Air Service to start the first aero engine repair organisation in the country. The tannery was equipped for the purpose, and Rootes, previously operating as a private firm, became Rootes Ltd, The Len Engineering Works, Maidstone, formed for the specific purpose of overhauling and repairing aero engines for the government. This view shows the Len Engineering Works shortly after the First World War.

Both male and female workers were engaged at the Works reconstructing Siddley-Puma, Le Rhone and B.H.P. aero engines, and for the following few months, with William at the helm, Rootes Ltd made a great contribution to the war effort.

This photograph, taken at the Len Engineering Works, shows an 80 h.p. Le Rhone engine with wind break, mounted on a gun carriage for testing. The noise from the exhausts of these aero engines on test was deafening and caused many local inhabitants to complain.

When peace was declared William returned to the motor trade and persuaded his brother Reginald to relinquish his Civil Service career and join him at Mill Street. The brothers became joint managing directors of Rootes Ltd and the Company became Britain's largest motor retailer with distribution channels all over England. This photograph shows Rootes Ltd, Mill Street, in 1922 with ornamental archway to the garage, and car & accessory showrooms.

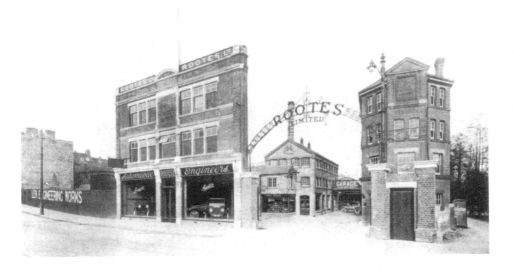

Rootes Ltd, Mill Street, decorated with flags for the Coronation of King George VI in May 1937. By this time Rootes controlled eight manufacturing companies, seven distributing companies and three financial and property companies, and were selling every kind of motor vehicle from luxury limousines to delivery vans, municipal vehicles, three-wheeled mechanical horses and trolleybuses. Rootes by then had one of the largest export businesses in the British motor industry.

The Electricity Showroom in the High Street, with the Rootes sign above, was one of the best illuminated buildings in the town at the time of the Coronation of King George VI.

In 1937/8 Rootes Ltd decided to rebuild the Len Engineering Works into a model super service station. The first section, the showrooms and office block, was opened by Messrs Rootes on 4th April 1938. This photograph dated 18th February 1938 and the following photograph dated the 4th March 1938, show the new Mill Street showrooms under construction. Between the two dates, the old showrooms were evacuated and totally demolished.

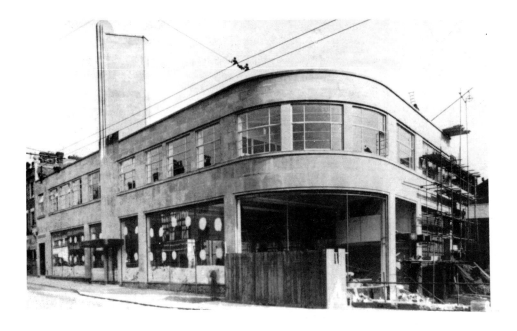

The new Rootes' Showrooms, with an overall floor area of 9,730 sq.ft, were, at that time, the largest and most up-to-date in Kent, and at night they were visible for miles around with no less than 700ft of Neon tubing outlining the frontage and the name 'Rootes' on the tower above the main entrance.

To mark the opening of the new showrooms, Rootes Ltd held a special Spring Motor Display, and in addition to fully representative ranges of Humber, Hillman and Talbot cars, and Commer and Karrier commercial vehicles, the display reflected every aspect of motoring. This photograph shows from left to right: William Rootes chatting with the Mayor of Maidstone, Councillor W.R. Hyde, and Alfred C. Bossom M.P. after the opening of the new showrooms. A Karrier A.R.P. trailer unit can be seen in the background.

In 1939 the former tannery buildings were pulled down to make way for new workshops, garages, administrative offices, spares sales department and stores. The chimney was demolished at 5 a.m. on 1st July 1939, but owing to the Second World War, Rootes' new Maidstone Service Station was not completed until 1st March 1941. Rootes Ltd was taken over by Chrysler in 1967 and subsequently by P.S.A., the French car giant controlling both Peugeot and Citroen. The Company is now called the Peugeot-Talbot Motor Company in the United Kingdom.

This small engineering shop in the Broadway at Maidstone belonged to the partners James A. Drake and Richard Muirhead who had, in 1876, set up machines for the repair of light domestic appliances, specialising in sewing machines. James Drake worked one of the lathes and Richard Muirhead took the lead in the management.

The partners later applied their talents to the production of farm appliances and, about 1885, James Drake invented this 'Drake Oil & Gas Engine' which was suitable for farm and estate work, hop and fruit tree spraying, hop drying, pumping and electric lighting. Many of these machines were still in use until the Second World War.

In 1890 James Drake left the firm and the business became a limited liability company, with the registered title of 'The Kent Engineering Works Ltd'. Richard Muirhead also had cause to leave the Company in 1897 and A.J. Fletcher, an enterprising employee who had joined the firm in 1889 as a junior clerk, acquired his share with a borrowed £500 and took over the business. James Drake rejoined him as his partner to manage the Works and in 1898 the name of the company was changed to Drake & Fletcher Ltd. Mr and Mrs Fletcher together with Mr and Mrs Drake and their families, each occupied one floor of 19 The Broadway, later to be used as Head Office. In 1900 the Company went into the motor trade and also entered the road haulage business. This postcard shows one of Drake & Fletcher's road haulage vehicles in 1919.

In the 1920s Drake & Fletcher became agents for General Motors of Detroit who supplied Chevrolet lorries and cars. When, in 1925, General Motors took over Vauxhall Motors Ltd and then Opel, the Company's motor business began to grow more rapidly. This Drake & Fletcher Bus was a 1926 Chevrolet X with a 14 seat charabanc body, built for W. Davis, St John's Hill, Sevenoaks.

Above
From 1931 General Motors supplied Bedford commercial vehicles. This photograph shows Drake & Fletcher's first nine Bedford vehicles, lined up outside the Broadway premises in June 1932. All were sold to G.J. Wright of Redhill, for a total cost of £2,420.27p.

Below
Another line up of Bedfords and Vauxhalls, in front of Drake & Fletcher's newly rebuilt premises in the Broadway in 1936, ready to be delivered to Charles Arkcoll Ltd, wholesale grocers at 27, 29, 31 & 33 Lower Stone Street.

The agricultural side of the business also grew steadily, supplying farmers with every kind of farm implement. This photograph shows a Gang Mower supplied by Drake & Fletcher Ltd in 1946. Kent's first hop picking machine was installed by Drake & Fletcher Ltd in 1953. In 1957 the firm was granted the Royal Warrant for supplying Agricultural Spraying Machinery to Her Majesty Queen Elizabeth II, and in 1977 was presented with a silver medal for giving the most outstanding service to the agricultural industry throughout the twenty-five years of the Queen's reign.

In 1972 Drake & Fletcher sold the old site in the Broadway; it is currently occupied by Waldron Ltd (specialist cars). With premises now at Rocky Hill, Tonbridge Road and Park Wood at Maidstone, and branches in other parts of Kent, Drake & Fletcher Ltd is one of the largest agricultural machinery distributors in the south-east and the only remaining producer of fruit and hop sprayers in the county. In parallel with the agricultural business, the motor and truck operations have also expanded over the years and the Company now offers cars from the Chevette to the Mercedes Benz and still supplies Bedford commercial vehicles. This Bedford lorry was delivered to Fremlin's Brewery by Drake & Fletcher Ltd in the 1950s.

This photograph shows Jesse Ellis, a traction engine operator, standing by one of his engines at Invicta Works & Sufferance Wharf, St Peter's Street, Maidstone, in the 1890s. He also had premises at Allington Works, London Road. Jesse Ellis started his business in Maidstone about 1870 and was a contractor for road haulage, the supply of road materials and the maintenance of roads. He later developed his own steam lorries but these were not a financial success and his company ceased trading in 1912. It is interesting to note that his telephone number was No. 2, Maidstone.

This postcard, photographed at the turn of the century, shows a local gang maintaining the roads using stone chippings and an Aveling and Porter Steam Roller, built in Rochester. Tarring the roads was not introduced until about 1910.

When Jesse Ellis vacated the Invicta Works in St Peter's Street in 1912, the firm of Edward Sharp & Co. purchased the property and built their new Kreemy Toffee Factory on the site. This Company had been founded by Edward Sharp in 1876 in a grocer's shop at 141 Week Street. He progressed first to the 'Cash Stores' at 93 Week Street, then to the former Maidstone Roller Skating Rink in Sandling Road where his famous Kreemy Toffee was first produced. This photograph shows another of Edward Sharp's specialities, Almond Cream Nougat, also manufactured at the Rink.

Edward Sharp also manufactured other products including baking powder, custard powder, lemonade powder and jellies which he delivered by bicycle to many parts of Kent. He progressed to a horse and cart and by 1913 had this fleet of vehicles, shown lined up outside the garages and stables at 57 St Peter's Street. There were two Hallford 4-ton motor vans, two smaller vans and six horse-drawn carts. A 4-ton Commer lorry was added to the fleet in 1915.

After the First World War, Sharp's introduced Super Kreem Toffee and with it appeared 'Sir Kreemy Knut', a dapper young fellow, with bowler hat, monocle and walking stick. The 'toff' appeared on most of Sharp's toffee tins, vehicles and advertisements. This photograph shows the 'toff' on the six new Tilling-Stevens petrol electric vehicles purchased by Edward Sharp & Co. Ltd in 1919. All in red livery, two were 4½ tons and four were 2½ tons.

This photograph shows a live 'Sir Kreemy Knut' on top of one of the new vans, only registered the previous day, leaving the prison wall in the Peace Procession on 19th July 1919. During that day in Mote Park every child had received a tin of toffees from Mr and Mrs Edward Sharp and a newly minted sixpence from Sir Marcus Samuel, Bart.

Edward Sharp started to take part in public life in 1919 when he was elected to the Maidstone Town Council as the Liberal councillor for Bridge Ward. From then on he became increasingly committed to civic duties and in 1920 his two sons were appointed joint managing directors of the Company. In 1922 a baronetcy was conferred on Edward Sharp.

47

The profits for 1920 were higher than ever before; the sales for the first time exceeded £1,000,000 and Sharp's became the largest manufacturer of toffee in the world. This photograph shows the firm's famous Super-Kreem Toffee being transported by river.

The factory was enlarged and the existing office block on the opposite side of St Peter's Street was erected. Throughout the early 'twenties advertisements appeared for extra female staff offering them regular work and high wages. This photograph shows Sharp's Confectionery Room at the Kreemy Works, St Peter's Street, about 1930.

Sharp's entry for the Maidstone Carnival in 1931. Note the macaw on his perch on top of the van. These birds were used by Sharp's in carnivals etc to attract extra publicity, and between events were housed in Maidstone Zoo. In January 1947 the Company was honoured by the granting of the Royal Warrant and the privilege of displaying the Royal Arms with the title 'By Appointment, Confectioners to His Majesty King George VI'. The Royal Warrant was again given in November 1955 after the accession of Queen Eliabeth II. In 1960 Sharp's amalgamated with Robertson and Woodcock Ltd, a London firm founded in 1907 to manufacture and market Trebor boiled sweets. The new Company, since renamed Trebor Ltd which now consists of Sharp's, Robertson & Woodcock, Printway Ltd, A.F. Moffat Ltd Clarnico, Maynards and many overseas companies, still manufacture confectionery in S Peter's Street, Maidstone.